I desire dyestless — will nothing fill the bill

Books by Robert Pinsky

Poetry

SADNESS AND HAPPINESS

AN EXPLANATION OF AMERICA

HISTORY OF MY HEART

THE WANT BONE

Prose

LANDOR'S POETRY

THE SITUATION OF POETRY

POETRY AND THE WORLD

THE WANT BONE

THE WANT BONE

ROBERT PINSKY

The Ecco Press, New York

The Ecco Press
26 West 17th Street
New York, NY 10011
Published simultaneously in Canada by
Penguin Books Canada Ltd., Ontario
Printed in the United States of America
FIRST PAPERBACK EDITION
Grateful acknowledgment is made to the editors of the following
publications, in which some of these poems appeared: *Agni
Review, American Poetry Review, Antæus, The New Republic,
The New Yorker, Paris Review, Poetry, Raritan, Representations,
Salmagundi, The Threepenny Review, Tikkun, Verse, Wigwag,
Yale Review.*

"The Refinery" was first published in *The English Language*
(Second Edition), edited by Leonard Michaels and Christopher
Ricks.

Library of Congress Cataloging-in-Publication Data
Pinsky, Robert.
The want bone / Robert Pinsky. — 1st ed.
I. Title.
PS3566.I54W36   1990   811′.54—dc20   89-17067

ISBN 0-88001-251-X

The text of this book is set in Electra.

Contents

From the Childhood of Jesus, 3

Memoir, 6

Window, 9

The Hearts, 10

The Want Bone, 14

Shiva and Parvati Hiding in the Rain, 15

The Uncreation, 17

Lament for the Makers, 20

Picture, 23

Icicles, 24

Visions of Daniel, 25

Pilgrimage, 29

Jesus and Isolt, 32

Immortal Longings, 41

Exile, 42

An Old Man, 43

What Why When How Who, 44

Voyage to the Moon, 49

Shirt, 53

The Night Game, 55

Sonnet, 58

Dreamer, 59

The Refinery, 60

Hut, 62

The Ghost Hammer, 65

At Pleasure Bay, 68

THE WANT BONE

from Apocryphal
Gospel of John

One Saturday morning he went to the river to play.
He modeled twelve sparrows out of the river clay

And scooped a clear pond, with a dam of twigs and mud.
Around the pond he set the birds he had made,

Evenly as the hours. Jesus was five. He smiled,
As a child would who had made a little world

Of clear still water and clay beside a river.
But a certain Jew came by, a friend of his father,

And he scolded the child and ran at once to Joseph,
Saying, "Come see how your child has profaned the Sabbath,

Making images at the river on the Day of Rest."
So Joseph came to the place and took his wrist

And told him, "Child, you have offended the Word."
Then Jesus freed the hand that Joseph held

And clapped his hands and shouted to the birds
To go away. They raised their beaks at his words

And breathed and stirred their feathers and flew away.
The people were frightened. Meanwhile, another boy,

4 ·   The son of Annas the scribe, had idly taken
       A branch of driftwood and leaning against it had broken

       The dam and muddied the little pond and scattered
       The twigs and stones. Then Jesus was angry and shouted,

       "Unrighteous, impious, ignorant, what did the water
       Do to harm you? Now you are going to wither

       The way a tree does, you shall bear no fruit
       And no leaves, you shall wither down to the root."

       At once, the boy was all withered. His parents moaned,
       The Jews gasped, Jesus began to leave, then turned

       And prophesied, his child's face wet with tears:
       "Twelve times twelve times twelve thousands of years

       Before these heavens and this earth were made,
       The Creator set a jewel in the throne of God

       With Hell on the left and Heaven to the right,
       The Sanctuary in front, and behind, an endless night

       Endlessly fleeing a Torah written in flame.
       And on that jewel in the throne, God wrote my name."

       Then Jesus left and went into Joseph's house.
       The family of the withered one also left the place,

       Carrying him home. The Sabbath was nearly over.
       By dusk, the Jews were all gone from the river.

       Small creatures came from the undergrowth to drink
       And foraged in the shadows along the bank.

Alone in his cot in Joseph's house, the Son   · 5
Of Man was crying himself to sleep. The moon

Rose higher, the Jews put out their lights and slept,
And all was calm and as it had been, except

In the agitated household of the scribe Annas,
And high in the dark, where unknown even to Jesus

The twelve new sparrows flew aimlessly through the night,
Not blinking or resting, as if never to alight.

Christianity gets in touch with more primitive
myths Judaism had repressed

The iron cape of the Law, the gray
Thumb of the Word:
Careless of the mere spirit, careless
Of the body, ardent
Elders of the passion of the soiled, the charred.

Snuffboxes, smells of Europe.
Mr. Sokol crooning blessings
Absently to himself,
Neither the words nor the music,
Nothing of the mind and nothing
Of the senses but only
That one thing that shall come to pass
If you will hearken diligently with all
Your heart and all your soul and lay up these,

My words, inside your heart and in your soul
And bind them as a sign upon your hand
And they will be as frontlets between your eyes:
So we wrote the words on squares of lambskin.

And we sealed them in wooden boxes bound
In leather and threaded the boxes
On black leather thongs and bound the thongs
With the sealed words in appointed places
Around our heads and arms.
It was like saying: I am this, and not that.

And you shall teach these words
To your children, boxes
Bound at the heart and the eyes,
And you shall speak of them when you sit
Inside your houses and when you stand
Speaking in the marketplace, and bound
In your heart entirely when you walk the avenues
And when you go to bed
And when you arise.

Tin canisters of money, tumblers
Of memorial wax.
Necktie of Poland, shirt of grief. Chickpeas
And Seagram's whiskey, blessings of mousefur lapels.
That, and not this.

And you shall fasten
These words onto your doorposts and your gates
And so we did, in boxes
Put for a sign and a memorial
To you upon your hands and at your eyes
And in your hearts and in your houses and so we wrapped
The thongs and boxes with words inside them
Around our hands and arms and heads
And wore them as frontlets between the eyes
Through the shadows of summer
With so many turns of leather
Around the fingers of the hand
Nearest the heart.
And when your son
Comes to you saying *what is this*
You shall tell him of the slaying
Of the firstborn of man and of beast
In Egypt when my father came out of Egypt. *Jesus writing*

Alien as a blue carapace and a trident.
Unreadable
Totems, gilt fringes, varnished books. A horse chestnut
Throwing its massive summer shade
Over the pavement.

But ye that did cleave
Unto the Lord your God are alive,
Every one of you, this day.
Smells of wool and chickpeas,
The sandstone building converted now
To a Puerto Rican Baptist church,
Clerestory and minaret.
A few blocks away, an immense blue
Pagan, an ocean, muttering, swollen:
That, and not this.

Ocean is pages
world on not of men
nature is amoral
not this and that
but nostalgia for clear cut
(even though catastrophic)

Our building floated heavily through the cold
On shifts of steam the raging coal-fed furnace
Forced from the boiler's hull. In showers of spark
The trolleys flashed careening under our cornice.
My mother Mary Beamish who came from Cork
Held me to see the snowfall out the window—
Windhold she sometimes said, as if in Irish
It held wind out, or showed us that wind was old.
Wind-hole in Anglo-Saxon: faces like brick,
They worshipped Eastre's rabbit, and mistletoe
That was Thor's jissom where thunder struck the oak.
We took their language in our mouth and chewed
(Some of the consonants drove us nearly crazy
Because we were Chinese—or was that just the food
My father brought from our restaurant downstairs?)
In the fells, by the falls, the Old Ghetto or New Jersey,
Little Havana or Little Russia—I forget,
Because the baby wasn't me, the way
These words are not. Whoever she was teaching to talk,
Snow she said, *Snow,* and you opened your small brown fist
And closed it and opened again to hold the reflection
Of torches and faces inside the window glass
And through it, a cold black sheen of shapes and fires
Shaking, kitchen lights, flakes that crissed and crossed
Other lights in lush diagonals, the snowcharmed traffic
Surging and pausing—red, green, white, the motion
Of motes and torches that at her word you reached
Out for, where you were, it was you, that bright confusion.

The legendary muscle that wants and grieves,
The organ of attachment, the pump of thrills
And troubles, clinging in stubborn colonies

Like pulpy shore-life battened on a jetty.
Slashed by the little deaths of sleep and pleasure,
They swell in the nurturing spasms of the waves,

Sucking to cling; and even in death itself—
Baked, frozen—they shrink to grip the granite harder.
"Rid yourself of attachments and aversions"—

But in her father's orchard, already, he says
He'd like to be her bird, and she says: Sweet, yes,
Yet I should kill thee with much cherishing,

Showing that she knows already—as Art Pepper,
That first time he takes heroin, already knows
That he will go to prison, and that he'll suffer

And knows he needs to have it, or die; and the one
Who makes the General lose the world for love
Lets him say, *Would I had never seen her*, but Oh!

Says Enobarbus, Then you would have missed
A wonderful piece of work, which left unseen
Would bring less glory to your travels. Among

The creatures in the rock-torn surf, a wave
Of agitation, a gasp. A scholar quips,
Shakespeare was almost certainly homosexual,

Bisexual, or heterosexual, the sonnets
Provide no evidence on the matter. He writes
Romeo an extravagant speech on tears,

In the Italian manner, his teardrops cover
His chamber window, says the boy, he calls them crystals,
Inanely, and sings them to Juliet with his heart:

The almost certainly invented heart
Which Buddha denounces, in its endless changes
Forever jumping and moving, like an ape.

Over the poor beast's head the crystal fountain
Crashes illusions, the cold salt spume of pain
And meaningless distinction, as Buddha says,

But here in the crystal shower mouths are open
To sing, it is Lee Andrews and The Hearts
In 1957, singing *I sit in my room*

Looking out at the rain, My tear drops are
Like crystals, they cover my windowpane, the turns
Of these illusions we make become their glory:

To Buddha every distinct thing is illusion
And becoming is destruction, but still we sing
In the shower. I do. In the beginning God drenched

The Emptiness with images: the potter
Crosslegged at his wheel in Benares market
Making mud cups, another cup each second

Tapering up between his fingers, one more
To sell the tea-seller at a penny a dozen,
And tea a penny a cup. The customers smash

The empties, and waves of traffic grind the shards
To mud for new cups, in turn; and I keep one here
Next to me: holding it awhile from out of the cloud

Of dust that rises from the shattered pieces,
The risen dust alive with fire, then settled
And soaked and whirling again on the wheel that turns

And looks on the world as on another cloud,
On everything the heart can grasp and throw away
As a passing cloud, with even Enlightenment

Itself another image, another cloud
To break and churn a salt foam over the heart
Like an anemone that sucks at clouds and makes

Itself with clouds and sings in clouds and covers
Its windowpane with clouds that blur and melt,
Until one clings and holds—as once in the Temple

In the time before the Temple was destroyed
A young priest saw the seraphim of the Lord:
Each had six wings, with two they covered their faces,

With two they covered their legs and feet, with two
They darted and hovered like dragonflies or perched
Like griffins in the shadows near the ceiling—

These are the visions, too barbarous for heaven
And too preposterous for belief on earth,
God sends to taunt his prophet with the truth

No one can see, that leads to who knows where.
A seraph took a live coal from the altar
And seared the prophet's lips, and so he spoke.

As the record ends, a coda in retard:
The Hearts in a shifting velvety *ah,* and *ah*
Prolonged again, and again as Lee Andrews

Reaches *ah* high for *I have to gain Faith, Hope*
And Charity, God only knows the girl
Who will love me—Oh! if we only could

Start over again! Then The Hearts chant the chords
Again a final time, *ah* and the record turns
Through all the music, and on into silence again.

*Buddhist - detachment, eliminates attachments + desires
doesn't like him*
*poetry always finding new objects and things to
be attached to.*
poets should be like lovers are
Judaism that barbarism wild

The tongue of the waves tolled in the earth's bell.
Blue rippled and soaked in the fire of blue.
The dried mouthbones of a shark in the hot swale
Gaped on nothing but sand on either side.

The bone tasted of nothing and smelled of nothing,
A scalded toothless harp, uncrushed, unstrung.
The joined arcs made the shape of birth and craving
And the welded-open shape kept mouthing O.

Ossified cords held the corners together
In groined spirals pleated like a summer dress.
But where was the limber grin, the gash of pleasure?
Infinitesimal mouths bore it away,

The beach scrubbed and etched and pickled it clean.
But O I love you it sings, my little my country
My food my parent my child I want you my own
My flower my fin my life my lightness my O.

HIDING IN THE RAIN

Language of invasion, cloth of grief.
*"How can I turn this wheel
that turns my life?"*

Plural, playful.
Coat of morning-glory petals, bracelet
Of summer shadows,

The double-budded god
Having their fill
Of themselves. She

Cupped in his lap
Both wrapped in one cloak
Her arm clasping his neck.

Supplicants come, torturers
And sufferers on the wheel
Soldiers and scholars

Artisans and lovers, with words,
Dungeon and fashion, passion
And onion, from Venice ghetto,

From Prague dollar, stitches
Of captivity, inherited
Eyecolor or ear for music

Of raper and raped. Also this,
Also that, coupled the pair
Barely listen, turning

To embrace beyond reason—
Each is also the other, in touching
Touched, also the threads

Of rain and also the wheel
Of the sky also the foliage
So delicate only the torn-off

Wings of the green woodbeetle
Could represent it in a picture:
The rosecolored mother-father

Flushed, full, penetrated and
Also penetrated, entering
And entering, endowing

And also devouring, necklace
Of skulls and also ecstasy
Of hiding in raindrops, in

The storm, their eight sleek
Limbs and numberless
Faces all spokes from one trunk.

The crowd at the ballpark sing, the cantor sings
Kol Nidre, and the equipment in our cars
Fills them with singing voices while we drive.

When the warlord hears his enemy is dead,
He sings his praises. The old men sang a song
And we protesters sang a song against them,

Like teams of children in a singing game;
And at the great convention all they did
They punctuated with a song: our breath

Which is an element and so a quarter
Of all creation, heated and thrown out
With all the body's force to shake our ears.

Everything said has its little secret song,
Strained higher and lower as talking we sing all day,
The sentences turned and tinted by the body:

A tune of certain pitch for questions, a tune
For *that was not a question,* a tune for *was it,*
The little tunes of begging, of coolness, of scolding.

The Mudheads dance in their adobe masks
From house to house, and sing at each the misdeeds
Of the small children inside. And we must take you,

They sing, Now we must take you, Now we must take
You back to the house of Mud. But then the parents
With presents for the Mudheads in their arms

Come singing each child's name, and buy him back:
Forgive him, give him back, we'll give you presents.
And the prancing Mudheads take the bribes, and sing.

I make a feeble song up while I work,
And sometimes even machines may chant or jingle
Some lyrical accident that takes its place

In the great excess of song that coats the world.
But after the flood the bland Immortals will come
As holy tourists to our sunken world,

To slide like sunbeams down shimmering layers of blue:
Artemis, Gog, Priapus, Jehovah and Baal,
With faces calmer than when we gave them names,

Walking our underwater streets where bones
And houses bloom fantastic spurts of coral,
Until they find our books. The pages softened

To a dense immobile pulp between the covers
Will rise at their touch in swelling plumes like smoke,
With a faint black gas of ink among the swirls,

And the golden beings shaping their mouths like bells
Will impel their breath against the weight of ocean
To sing us into the cold regard of water.

A girl sang dancing once, and shook her hair.
A young man fasting to have a powerful dream
Sang as he cut his body, to please a spirit.

But the Gods will sing entirely, the towering spumes
Dissolving around their faces will be the incense
Of their old anonymity restored

In a choral blast audible in the clouds,
An immense vibration that presses the very fish,
So through her mighty grin the whale will sing

To keep from bursting, and the tingling krill
Will sing in her jaws, the whole cold salty world
Humming oblation to what our mouths once made.

What if I told you the truth? What if I could?
The nuptial trek of the bower apes in May:
At night in the mountain meadow their clucking cries,

The reeking sulphur springs called Smoking Water,
Their skimpy ramparts of branches, pebbles and vines—
So slightly better than life, that snarl of weeds,

The small-town bank by comparison is Rome,
With its four-faced bronze clock that chimes the hours,
The six great pillars surmounted by a frieze

Of Cronus eating his children—or trying to,
But one child bests him because we crave to live,
And if that too means dying then to die

Like Arthur when ladies take him in his barge
Across the misty water: better than life,
Or better than truly dying. In the movies

Smoking and driving are better, a city walk.
Grit on the sidewalk after a thaw, mild air.
I took the steps along the old stone trestle

Above the station, to the part of town
I never knew, old houses flush to the street
Curving uphill. Patches of ice in the shade.

What if I found an enormous secret there
And told you? We would still feel something next
Or even at the same time. Just as now. In Brooklyn,

Among the diamond cutters at their benches
Under high Palladian windows full of a storm,
One wearing headphones listens to the Talmud.

What if he happens to feel some saw or maxim
Inwardly? Then the young girl in her helmet,
An allegorical figure called The Present,

Would mime for us the action of coming to life:
A crease of shadow across her face, a cross,
And through the window, washing stumps of brick,

Exuberant streaks and flashes—literal lightning
Spilling out into a cheery violent rain.
Worship is tautological, with its Blessed

Art thou O Lord who consecrates the Sabbath
Unto us that we may praise it in thy name
Who blesses us with this thy holy day

That we may hallow it unto thy holy blessings. . . .
And then the sudden curt command or truth:
God told him, Thou shalt cut thy foreskin off.

Then Abraham was better than life. The monster
Is better when he startles us. Hurt is vivid,
Sincerity visible in the self-inflicted wound.

Paws bleeding from their terrible climb, they weave
Garlands of mountain creeper for their bed.
The circle of desire, that aches to play

Or sings to hear the song passing. We sense
How much we might yet make things change, renewed
As when the lovers rise from their bed of play

And dress for supper and from a lewd embrace
Undress again. Weeds mottle the fissured pavement
Of the playground in a net of tufted lines

As sunset drenches a cinematic honey
Over the stucco terraces, copper and blue,
And the lone player cocks wrist and ball behind

His ear and studies the rusty rim again.
The half-ruined city around him throbs and glows
With pangs of allure that flash like the names of bars

Along San Pablo Avenue: Tee Tee's Lounge,
The Mallard Club, Quick's Little Alaska, Ruthie's,
Chiquita's, and inside the sweet still air

Of tobacco, malt and lime, and in some music
But in others only voices or even quiet,
And the player's arm pauses and pumps again.

Three men on scaffolding scatter cornflakes down
For people to see in black-and-white as snow,
Falling around the actor under the lights.

The actor hunches in the flakes, the set
Is a bitter street, the camera dollies in
And the monster stamps and sorrows, now he's lost,

He shakes his arms and howls, an ugly baby,
Nostrils forced open by little makeup springs.
The dust of cornflakes, trampled underfoot,

Infiltrates his lungs, he starts to wheeze
And so they take a break and start again.
Weeks later, he dies of pneumonia, maybe by chance—

But the picture is finished, people see the scene
And if they know, they feel the extra pathos,
Even if they joke a little about it. The movie

Is silent, cornflakes are a kind of health food,
It's all that long ago, although the picture
Survives as flecks of light and dark on substances

Not invented when they made it—or a play
Of information, a magnetic mist
Of charges, particles too fine to see.

A brilliant beard of ice
Hangs from the edge of the roof
Harsh and heavy as glass.
The spikes a child breaks off

Taste of wool and the sun.
In the house, some straw for a bed,
Circled by a little train,
Is the tiny image of God.

The sky is a fiery blue,
And a fiery morning light
Burns on the fresh deep snow:
Not one track in the street.

Just as the carols tell
Everything is calm and bright:
The town lying still
Frozen silver and white.

Is only one child awake,
Breaking the crystal chimes? —
Knocking them down with a stick,
Leaving the broken stems.

Magician, appointed officer
Of the crown. He thrived, he never
Seemed to get older.

Golden curly head.
Smooth skin, unreadable tawny eyes,
Former favorite, they said,
Of the chief eunuch of Nebuchadnezzar,
Who taught him the Chaldean language and courtly ways
And gave him his name of a courtier:
"Daniel who was called Belteshazzar"
In silk and Egyptian linen.
Proprietor, seer.

The Jews disliked him,
He smelled of pagan incense and char.
Pious gossips in the souk
Said he was unclean,
He had smeared his body with thick
Yellowish sperm of lion
Before he went into the den,
The odor and color
Were indelible, he would reek
Of beast forever.

Wheat-color. Faint smell as of smoke.
The Kings of Babylon feared him
For generations.

And Daniel who was called in Chaldean
Belteshazzar, meaning spared-by-the-lion
Said as for thee O King I took
Thy thoughts into my mind
As I lay upon my bed: You saw O King a great
Image with His head of gold His heart
And arms of silver His belly and thighs of brass
His legs of iron His feet
Part of iron and part of clay
And then alas
O Nebuchadnezzar the image fell

And clay and iron
And brass and gold and silver
Lay shattered like chaff on the
Threshingfloor in summer.

Terrified Nebuchadnezzar
Went on all fours, driven
To eat grass like the oxen.
His body wet by the dews of heaven,
Hair matted like feathers, fingers
Hooked like the claw of the raven.

Interpreter, survivor,
Still youthful years later
When Nebuchadnezzar's son Belshazzar
Saw a bodiless hand
Scrawl meaningless words on the plaster
Mene Tekel Upharsin,
Interpreted by Daniel, You are finished,
God has weighed you and found you
Wanting, your power will be given
To the Medes and the Persians.

And both King Darius the Mede
And King Cyrus the Persian
Feared him and honored him.

Yellow smoking head,
High royal administrator.
Unanointed. He declined
To bow to images.

Then one night God sent him a vision
Of the world's entire future
Couched in images: The lion
With the wings of an eagle
And feet of a man, the bear
With the mouth in its side
That said, Devour Much Flesh,
The four-headed leopard
Of dominion, and lastly
The beast with iron teeth
That devoured and broke
And stamped and spat
Fiery streams before him.

And he wrote, I the Jew Daniel
Saw the horn of the fourth beast
Grow eyes and a mouth and the horn
Made war with the saints and
Prevailed against them.

Also, he saw a man clothed in linen
Who stood upon the waters
And said, As to the abomination
And the trial and the making white
Go thy way O Daniel, for the words
Are closed up and sealed till the end.

For three weeks after this night vision
I Daniel, he wrote, ate no pleasant
Bread nor wine, my comeliness
Turned to corruption, I retained
No strength, my own countenance
Changed in me. But I kept the
Matter in my heart, I was mute
And set my face toward the earth.
And afterward I rose up
And did the king's business.

Appalled initiate. Intimate of power.
Scorner of golden images, governor.
In the drinking places they said
He had wished himself unborn,
That he had no navel.

So tawny Belteshazzar or Daniel
With his unclean smell of lion
And his night visions,
Who took the thoughts of the King
Into his mind O Jews, prospered
In the reign of Nebuchadnezzar
And of his son Belshazzar
And in the reign of Darius
And the reign of Cyrus the Persian.

Near the peak. A clear morning,
Camphorous air of eucalyptus and mountain laurel
Lining the steep trail.

They chant in chorus as they climb,
Some of them in turns bearing
The ark—its hammered silver
Ornaments jangling, the pressure
Of polished cedar beams heavily
Afloat on their shoulders,
The others reaching in
To touch it as they dance and kiss
Their fingers that brushed it.

At the last of the dusty switchbacks
The trail grows wider and flatter
And they pause, flushed and shuffling.
They lower the ark to the earth,
A priest singing his aria
From beside it: Now I call you by your
True name—and they come forward:

One by one he fits
Embroidered blinders over their eyes
And guiding them singly by the hand
Singing the secret name of each
He leads them from the ark upward

To the cliff's edge, till the whole choir
Stands dancing in place
At the precipice, each man and woman
Chanting in a darkness.

At the prayer's end
They lift the blinders
To see the falls across the sheer vacancy:

Mountain light, the bridal veil
Skimming the great vertical
Rockface without interval,
Unquenchable granite in its plumage
Of air and falling water:
                    O Presence
You have searched me and seen me from afar,
My downsitting and my uprising.
Now nothing is next or before, there is
Nothing yet to enter, you have beset me
Behind and before, you have put
Your hand upon me, though I am
Fearfully and wonderfully made,
You have known me from afar.

Now for many of them
The falls appear motionless: hung
From the foamless brim in a vision
Of suspended flowing, falling
But unfallen. Through tears
Of pleasure they squint upward.

Now when they take the thick wizened scroll
Out from the ark in its white armor
And unfurl it, the crowned letters
Scorched and stained into the skin

In a catalogue of secret names —
                    Akhman, Ruveyne,
Yeosif, each sound indicated by characters
That form another sound, never to be uttered,
And behind each unutterable name
The name of that name's
Name in infinite regress —

They read themselves into the unchangeable
Book of the journey begun before
Your body was called up
And before it was made,
Before you were a seed packed in honey, before you

Fell from the brim, fashioned and torn
From the cold water that tumbles
Endlessly down the face of the mountain.

In the palace of Heaven God's holy angels were touching and fondling one another, gently and mutually, just as St. Augustine says they do, and laving their hair with oil of myrrh. But the Lord Jesus watched them with a scowl.

He said to his Mother, who sat on her throne of pearl, "Divinity is a leash to me, I miss the unquenchable days of living and dying, my old quarrels and victories among the Jews—I won't be bound by my own nature."

Mild and flawless Mary smiled and with her small white hand stroked Jesus' brow in a gesture of permission. So Jesus left the company of the Virgin and her angels and abandoned his divine form. His Mother gave him a pair of soft gray leathery wings, and a compact furry body with strong haunches and gloved forepaws like a raccoon's. In the form of a ciclogriff, with his divine eyes gazing from above the severe beak of an eagle, Jesus flew down to earth.

He flew down through the cool aethereal stars of heaven and past the fiery material stars of creation, and down through the clouds of a night sky over the North Sea. The black ocean churned and tilted under him. Swells of wind caught his wings and sent him careening through the night. Jesus felt the cold air split over his clenched beak, riffling through his fur, and the joyful pulse of risk and adventure was restored in him. With unfaltering wing strokes he brought himself down to the tower over the surf where Isolt stood at the railing wrapped in her cloak, looking out over the waves.

At first Isolt thought that the creature flapping down to her side was a seabird blown from its perch, or a bat from its cave in the cliffs that rose beachless from the waves. The ciclogriff shuddered water from its outspread wings and folded them around its body. Then like a tame rabbit it hopped quietly to Isolt's side. When the creature laid its beak against her knee and stretched its neck to look up into her face, Isolt petted it. She let her hand rest on the ciclogriff's round furry head, and with a finger traced the cool surface of his beak, while she looked out at the water where Tristram had sailed.

· · ·

In many of the oldest illustrations of the story of Tristram and Isolt, the ciclogriff can be seen in this pose, his head resting against the side of Isolt's leg. In some representations, he stares back at the viewer with bold intelligence. In some he is portrayed, inaccurately, with birdlike webbed feet or claws rather than furry paws. Because of the batlike wings visible in all versions, and the handlike forepaws, some scholars have taken the figure of the ciclogriff to signify the spirits of Hell to which the lovers are doomed, or a mystic familiar, a symbol of the magical powers Isolt inherited from her mother.

That the little creature was in fact a latter incarnation of our Saviour Jesus Christ was not revealed even to Isolt herself, although the ciclogriff did often speak to her, during their many long nights together, of his days among the Jews in the time of Jesus. In Cornwall and in Wales and even as a child in Ireland, she had seen Jewish peddlers and scribes. Jewish settlements were common in the south and west of Britain, dark warrens of huts and workshops where the Jews sold trinkets and precious gems, rare manuscripts and absurd ballads. For Isolt, the Jews were exotic creatures like Gypsies, and in childhood lore the descendants of the betrayers of Jesus.

The ciclogriff spoke to Isolt of political and religious factions in the dynasties of the Herods and the Maccabees, of the struggles between the Pharisees and the Sadducees, and of King Herod Antipas's ploys to appear sufficiently Jewish in the eyes of the populace. He told her of the bottomless intrigues amongst the families of the ten wives of Herod the Great, the incests and fratricides and infanticides and parricides in the great ruling houses, Jewish and part Jewish and Pagan. By the fire at night, or through the long afternoons in the palace of King Mark, always within earshot of the thundering and sighing waves, Isolt thinking constantly of Tristram distracted herself with the strange stories of the ciclogriff.

In turn, Jesus asked Isolt about the movements and sensations of romantic love. First, shy even in the presence of the little beaked creature, she told him about the intertwining of love and wounds. She recounted the story of how Tristram arrived in Ireland by ship, with his harp and his wound, and how Isolt's mother the sorceress nursed him to health, only to find the chipped place in Tristram's sword that matched the fragment that was embedded in the brainpan of Sir Marhaus the brother of Isolt's mother and the champion of Ireland.

The ciclogriff looked up at Isolt with his grave intelligent eyes, and she told him about Tristram's harp and his voice. She told him about Tristram's reckless courage in battle, the terrible gashes and punctures he had sustained by sword and by lance, his deep honor and his disdain for public glory. She told the story of the Irish dragon that terrified her home country and that nearly killed Tristram, who finally cut off the monster's head and left it smoking on the ground, taking with him only the dragon's black tongue that he cut off as a trophy. The Seneschal found the dragon's head and carried it into court claiming that he had severed it in battle. The Seneschal was exposed and shamed when the missing tongue was found hanging by a silver chain from Tristram's armor, along with a bit of blue ribbon from Isolt's gown.

For nearly a year the ciclogriff remained in Cornwall attending Isolt, walking the ramparts with her or talking in her chamber, where she kept herself apart from King Mark. Because God the Father had made Jesus love all humankind with a boundless and impartial mercy, the ciclogriff could not fall in love with the fair Isolt, but he was moved by the passionate and confused course of her life, by her beauty, and by the artless, obsessive way she told her story. He amused her and shocked her with his stories of the cunning and ambitious generals and whores and priests of Judaea. Once, Isolt thought to ask him if he had seen our Lord and Saviour Jesus Christ.

"I was there," said the ciclogriff, "at His trial and at His mortifica-
tion. I was there when they crucified Him."

As always, it was impossible to tell from Isolt's face and voice if she
believed what the ciclogriff said. "When they put the crown of thorns
on His head," she asked, "and when they mocked Him and scourged
Him?"

"Yes."

"And what was the bearing of Our Lord, what did you read in His
face?"

"He knew them. He knew them through and through, Jew, Roman
and Greek. Jesus was like someone who has already won the contest or
stored up his profit. He was the Victor, and as the Victor He pitied
them."

As Isolt grew less shy, she told the ciclogriff in detail about the
pleasures and hurts of love between a man and a woman. She
described how two people become as one, without shame or conceal-
ment. Over the months she recounted the trysts and separations, the
vows and losses, of her life with Tristram. For all this Jesus felt pity,
but also a gratifying sense of reliving his own drama, the struggle for
which he had come. In Isolt's almost childish accounts of the effects
upon her of the love potion she had swallowed, in the heedless
contradictions and paradoxes of the behavior of the two lovers in Isolt's
own account, the Son of Man felt something that eased the restless-
ness of his own double nature. At times, it was as if he walked the
streets of Jerusalem again, defying the Sanhedrin by curing the blind
on the Sabbath.

·　　　·　　　·

Then one day Tristram appeared, and carried Isolt away. Like a storm
from the sea he sailed up one morning and broke through the castle's
defenses, and leaving a trail of blood he carried her away as he had
before. The ciclogriff awoke to the cries of the wounded and the
agitated sounds of the castle resounding to King Mark's helpless rage.
Jesus took wing immediately. From the bright, icy height of a cloud-

less sky he spotted the sails of Tristram's ship. Within minutes he was on board, and in the cabin of the lovers.

When Jesus Christ, in the shape of the ciclogriff, first looked on Tristram of Lyonesse, Tristram was thirty-eight years of age, a tall, bull-necked and scar-covered killer and harper. Tristram was wearing a sleeveless linen sleeping gown cut off at his battlemarked thighs, which resembled the twisted and mutilated boles of a double oak. Tristram's yellow hair, streaked with gray, fell to his shoulders. One scar crossed his boyish face from his left temple to the corner of his mouth, and his body was a maze of puckered lines and pale indentations. In his arms was a blue harp.

Tristram had been playing and singing to Isolt when the sailors brought Jesus to his cabin, and he resumed singing almost immediately. In a sweet high tenor, almost a counter-tenor, Tristram sang the improbable and violent stories of chivalry. In the course of his first time on earth, Jesus had known many soldiers and violent men: professional killers, practical thieves, uncontrolled brutes. But nothing in that adult, Romanized world prepared him for the solemnly choreographed, pedantically structured brutality of chivalric combat. The boyish code of knighthood fascinated the Saviour, with its heroes who hacked at one another all afternoon, according to rules immutable as the musical scales, making the ground slippery with blood, and then kissed and swore promises and escorted one another to chapels to be confessed by suffragans.

Isolt listened calmly, her head resting on Tristram's chest and one hand toying with the long fur at the ciclogriff's nape, her matchless face full of contentment, while the knight sang in his high voice of his bloody battles with Sir Palamides, the sad strokes they each received, the blows that brought them bleeding to one knee or groveling to the earth, the challenges and maimings and courtesies. The ciclogriff, with his experience of triumph in the receiving of blows, listened with strange compassion to the grave, sweet self-celebrations of Tristram, doomed to defeat and loss in his skill at the giving of blows.

Conversely, all that the ciclogriff told of the intrigues and abominations of Judaea Tristram converted into poems of lofty and stylized

combat. The intricate, subtle treachery of Herod Antipas, the hy-
pocrisies bequeathed by Marc Antony to corrupt governors and
wheedling catamites, perfected by rulers who as a matter of policy
assassinated their sons and wives and mothers and grandmothers,
Tristram took from the hooked beak of the ciclogriff and returned as
highminded, repetitious lays and poems of preposterous beauty. Sir
Antipas and Lady Herodias and Sir Pontius Pilate himself were led by
the harp of Tristram through the naive, murderous dance of loyalty
and honor. Tristram thanked the ciclogriff for bringing him new
material for his poetry.

The Jewish soul of Jesus, pragmatic, ethical, logical, found in the
passionate and self-defeating codes of romantic love and knightly
combat some of what he lacked in the jeweled pavilions of Heaven. He
sailed with Tristram and Isolt to the far coast of Ireland and the Gard
Obscure. Tristram trained the ciclogriff to skip and dart over the
mighty two-edged sword as Tristram whirled and flashed it through
the air. Two or three times, at jousts and tournaments, Jesus rode in a
velvet pouch slung from Isolt's sidesaddle, and watched Tristram put
aside the blue harp in order to maim and butcher the flower of Irish
youth—from horseback with his lance, or on foot with sword and
mace.

Once, Tristram returned from an expedition, half raid and half
courtly gesture, to a neighboring fiefdom. The knight was exhilarated
and wounded, blood pumping through his chainmail from a deep
gash in his side. Isolt bathed the wound in barkwater and dressed it
with herbs and linen. The next day the hero, still a little feverish and
overexcited, came limping into Isolt's chamber, harp in hand, and
found the ciclogriff on her lap. Playfully, Tristram cuffed at the little
creature with his free hand. The ciclogriff raised its dainty paw and
caught Tristram's wrist, arresting the blow with the strength of an iron
bar. Tristram looked thoughtfully into the calm, intelligent gaze of
Jesus for a moment. Then he shrugged, like a man who has stepped
on his dog's tail, causing it to growl.

That day, Tristram sang his poem of the brothers Sir Helios and Sir
Helakos, who fell upon Sir Palamides, cursing him as a Saracen and

the two attacking him both at once. And Sir Palamides said that he trusted to die as good a Christian man as either brother, and that either they or he should be left dead in that place. And they rode over him, and lashed him many sad blows back and forth, until desperately he struck Sir Helakos dead through his shield. And then Sir Helios waxed strong, and doubled his strokes, and drove Sir Palamides endlong down the field and onto one knee, before the people of the city, who marveled that after so many wounds Sir Palamides could stand even on his knee. And hearing the people of the city, Sir Palamides spoke shame to himself, and lunged up and struck Sir Helios in the grated visage of his armor so that he fell to the ground groveling, whereat Sir Palamides darted up to him lightly and lashed off his helmet and smote him a blow that parted his head from his body.

·   ·   ·

A few weeks after Tristram sang this poem in praise of his old enemy Palamides, before the fair Isolt and Our Lord Jesus Christ in the shape of a ciclogriff, Tristram and Isolt were parted for the last time in life. Tristram left the Gard Obscure at the request of Arthur, and King Mark came and took what was his. The ciclogriff sailed with Isolt back to Tintagil, where he had first found her, and he would have liked to have talked as in the old days. But though she was affectionate, and kept the creature near her, Isolt took on a new custom of prolonged silences. In silence, while she stood at the rail or sat by the fire apart from the King, the ciclogriff held his beak at her knee in the old way.

Then one day word came that Sir Tristram was sick, and Isolt with a grant from Arthur that King Mark dare not deny sailed with her poultices and herbs to try to heal him as he had been healed by the arts of her mother years before. When she came into the room where Tristram lay dead by spite and trickery, the ciclogriff padded briskly at Isolt's heels. He remained at her side as she pressed a last kiss on the scar that crossed Tristram's face, and fell dead herself.

When Tristram and Isolt came together to the Gates of Hell, the ciclogriff was trotting at her side. He looked up at the towering ebony gates, the carved posts wider than five men could span, the black doors like tall cliffs, carved all over with obscenities and tortures, putti brutalized by centaurs, aged rabbis forced by centurions to defile the Torah, the mass boilings and incinerations of the damned, packed writhing into kettles and ovens. Jesus could see the seams and mends in the doors where he had burst the gates apart when he went down into the depths and harrowed the infernal spirits. He smiled to see that Satan had improvised ornamental buttresses and scenes of atrocity to cover the cracks where the gateposts of Hell had burst under the Saviour's blows.

Then Jesus turned to Isolt where she and Tristram stood before the gates and shed his form of a ciclogriff and revealed himself to her as he was in the garden of Gethsemane. With his human hand he stayed her and he told Tristram and Isolt that he was their Lord and Saviour Jesus Christ, who had been with them in the false shape of the ciclogriff. Urgently he called them to renounce their false attachments and their sins, and to follow him into the Kingdom of Heaven. In his clipped, all but cryptic manner of old, the Son of Man spoke hurriedly of the confusions and half-truths of their lives. Shedding tears of compassion, he lifted his hand to heal their blindness, and the hand glowed as if on fire, and his tears glowed, throwing the mysterious light of his truth over the Gates of Hell.

Isolt showed no surprise when the ciclogriff revealed himself as the Lord Jesus, though he felt that she listened intently to his words. Her beauty appeared more profound in the light of his raised hand and his tears. She seemed about to respond to Jesus, but the gates opened and Tristram deep in the habit of his old ways had already turned impatiently to descend into the fiery pit, with his foolish harp in his hand and his immense, futile sword hanging at his side. Instantly Isolt took his hand and they went down together into the pit.

·　　　·　　　·

The Gates of Hell banged shut and Jesus with nothing else to do turned his back on them. He climbed up through the deep caves of the earth and through the burning planets and stars of the material world.

He looked down as he passed over Tintagil in Cornwall and the Gard Obscure in the West of Ireland, and in the Holy Land over Nazareth and Galilee, and over Golgotha, the Place of Skulls. He flew on, up through the cool eternal stars of Heaven, until he reached the throne of his Mother, the Holy Virgin. There he looked into the mild eyes of Mary, who looked back with heavenly pity at the Son of Man, the most unfortunate of all his Father's creatures.

Inside the silver body
Slowing as it banks through veils of cloud
We float separately in our seats

in a plane

Like the cells or atoms of one
Creature, needs
And states of a shuddering god.

Under him, a thirsty brilliance.
Pulsing or steady,
The fixed lights of the city

And the flood of carlights coursing
Through the grid: Delivery,
Arrival, Departure. Whim. Entering

And entered. Touching
And touched: down
The lit boulevards, over the bridges

And the river like an arm of night.
Book, cigarette. Bathroom.
Thirst. Some of us are asleep.

We tilt roaring
Over the glittering
Zodiac of intentions.

E X I L E

Every few years you move
From one city to another
As if to perform this ritual.
Pictures to arrange, and furniture,

Cartons of books to shelve—
And here, bundled in newspaper,
Memory's mortal tokens, treasure
Of a life unearthed:

Clouded honey, seizures
Of hopelessness and passion,
Good nights or bad ones,
Days of minor victories and scars

Tasting of silver or iron.
Touch, loss, shouts, arts,
Gestures, whispers,
Helpless violence of sensation

Like rain flailing a window—
Then a clap of light, the body blinded
You could not say whether by
Restitution or disaster,

Clarified by tears and thunder.
Now you begin. For an instant
Everything reassures you
The long exile is over.

Back in a corner, alone in the clatter and babble
An old man sits with his head bent over a table
And his newspaper in front of him, in the cafe.

Sour with old age, he ponders a dreary truth—
How little he enjoyed the years when he had youth,
Good looks and strength and clever things to say.

He knows he's quite old now: he feels it, he sees it,
And yet the time when he was young seems—was it?
Yesterday. How quickly, how quickly it slipped away.

Now he sees how Discretion has betrayed him,
And how stupidly he let the liar persuade him
With phrases: *Tomorrow. There's plenty of time. Some day.*

He recalls the pull of impulses he suppressed,
The joy he sacrificed. Every chance he lost
Ridicules his brainless prudence a different way.

But all these thoughts and memories have made
The old man dizzy. He falls asleep, his head
Resting on the table in the noisy cafe.

The lovers love the boardwalk, the games of chance
And the cheap bright treats, booths and indifferent surf,
The old conspiracy of gain and pleasure

Flowering in the mind greedily to build the world
And break it. In the city, steel cords twitch a girder
Onto its fittings as the tower grows

Amid a pool of dwellings made from its litter—
Crate or abandoned dumpster, some built with reckless
Improvisation framelessly from tires,

Scrapwood and hammered cans. One room or dormer
Is a gutted TV set: a hollowed console
Large enough for a body, with a curtain

Hung neatly in the screen. Somewhere but where
Inside this body, infinitesimal keys
Brush over their tumblers in the oily dark

To stir the mysteries, Love and Work, we have made
And that make us willing to die for them—
That make us bleed, embodied maybe in codes,

Spurts of pressure and crucial variations
In the current of the soul, that lives by changing.
He liked her knees, her taste and smell. She thought

About the night they walked home over the snow,
The sound of presence itself crunching and squeaking
Under their boots in the abandoned streets,

Their bodies under their coats when they stopped to hug.
What do the lovers want? And we, do we prefer
The ocean or the snow? Or page sixteen

Of *Naughty Nurses*? What is it we need to feel
The other feels, to fill our wants? One man
Wanted to have a woman while she was drowning,

To have her feel him inside her when she drowned,
So when his family were away, he killed
A woman he paid, bound helpless in the tub.

We can enrich the scene around the crane
By imagining a lunchtime song and dance:
A gang of children from the shanties perform

To a tape machine, dancing and chanting along
An octave higher to supplement the machine's
Overworked speaker. Its regular distortion

Pulses like drumbrushes as they shuffle and skip,
Swinging their hips and clapping. A key keeps turning,
The tumblers falling to their inertial state:

Heavy equipment will clear away the warrens
That stream around the Cyclone fence, to grow
Again like weeds; though for now the builders applaud

And pass a few dollars through the silver fence
From where they eat their sandwiches in the shade
While the children caper. Or say the lovers smile

And give them money too, because it charms them
Or pleases us. The poor whore only wanted
The money, she was young, she meant to live.

But now a camera charms us, it has caught
Ballplayers miming instruments in the dugout:
One tootling a bat held out like a clarinet,

One strumming, another puffing a bat-bassoon,
The uniformed players playing, as in a Bacchic
Procession. When we buried the old man,

To do it right we had to stop seven times
As we walked toward the grave, to lower the body
Inside its box down to rest on the earth

And pray and lift it up again, each prayer
Functioning as a pause by which to show
Our sevenfold resistance, refusing haste.

And when we mourners do the actual work
Of shoveling the earth in, each taking a turn
With the one shovel, we must not pass the shovel

From hand to hand, but take it standing from earth
And shovel, then stab it back to where it stood.
The lovers live by the exacting rules

And discipline of their folly, they are without
Earnestness or hypocrisy, they are useless.
They don't say anything about the poor,

Or exchange scorn for the President, they are like
The dying poet who could not fix his attention
On approaching World War II, because he felt

Distracted by a girl. They cannot pay attention
To their food, whole centuries of suffering children
Are as nothing to them, and even while they speak

They barely listen, but trembling scribble an image
Of one another inside, stanzas or cartoons.
Even at the end of the world each lover searches

The eyes in the mirror of eyes to find an object
That is still snagged far down among the dark
Roots that grow tangled in the bottomless wells

Of our invention, the waters that pull downward
And drink up every motion of mind and body,
Agonized hunger for What Why When How Who—

More images, as when desiring we desire
Fresh musics of desire, at concentric removes.
Doing a brake job, he sings into the wheel

Somewhere alone she knows a boy is waiting
Ta da ta da ta da, So she drives on through
The night anticipating, because he makes

Her feel the way she used to feel, and so
While he rebuilds the calipers he makes
Me feel the music of her heart as she

Drives toward the boy whose waiting she imagines
Restoring her lost desire, concentric rings
Each seeing more than the one that it encloses

Yet somehow larger than what we make around it,
With even the death camps radiating their jargon
And nicknames, surrounded by their lore and studies

As the tumblers fall. The current swells and shifts,
It lives by changing—Andreas Capellanus
Eight hundred years ago, *The Art of Love:*

Rule IV: *It is well known that love is always
Increasing or decreasing.* The country changes
Outside of town, and the little town itself

Is so demolished it seems that all along
It was a tissue of changes, though the boardwalk
Still with its giddy herringbone ribbon marks

Our element at its border with a greater one,
That in its darkness regularly roars
And falls and rises: as if we made a rocket

Molded in the image of a human body
Hugging its shoulders, head at the streaming prow
With eyes held shut, and launched it at the sun.

*hunger of the eye for all some
aboriginal thing that it never sees*

*"Aggression; the strife of desire; the monstrous overbuilding
of the imagination; all the maze of displacement and
sublimation—if the soul in its fatigue should conceive some
arcadia devoid of all this fevered construction, then our first
footstep there would infect and repopulate that lunar
terrain."*

Raquel the Queen of Diamonds and La Hire
The One-Eyed Jack of Hearts have crossed a bridge
Of weathered stone, from the Old Town to the New,

Which is itself so old the houses lean
Drowsily under their crowns of thatch. They have
Coffee on the terrace of an inn that looks

Out over the canal: lawn, ducks, the towpath,
And in the distance beyond the hilly streets,
Turrets and pennants, and puffs of cloud. The pack

Of cards in their expectant, somewhat embarrassed
Silence are waiting for what will happen next,
Or for the story to go deeper in—

La Hire with his painted hatchet and leaf, Raquel
With her bouquet of poppies. There was a woman
Who worked in sweatshops or sewing piecework at home

To support her daughter and herself. The child
Spent hours alone inventing games of cards
Based on Casino and the Death of Arthur,

Or on Disney, the brothers Grimm and the game of War.
She gave them voices, and played against herself.
And later when she grew up and was a sculptor

She made a series of works with heavy limbs
Of smooth black metal, muscled and stenciled gold
With leaves and filigrees like the stiff black arm

Of her mother's old-fashioned sewing machine.
And one work in particular was titled
La Blaine du Var, after her favorite card,

A little dog portrayed by the Three of Spades
And named in the private French the child invented.
Raquel and her friend Argine the Queen of Clubs

Had won the dog in a struggle with Oscarre,
The Suicide King who holds his sword at his head:
She gave his name to an eight-foot work with chrome

Sinews and targets welded among the tangle
Of gilded black. Meanwhile the pair of court cards
Have clambered into the wicker gondola,

Already they are lifted above the earth
By the silken gaudy bulb of a balloon
Painted in the yellow and red of their brocades

With arcs of scallops, and lozenges of blue.
They steer it with a treadle and a fan.
But the cards were flat, their passion to be lifted

Became too light for her, she wanted the earth
Made sweeter by the feel of the weight that presses
Against it when it comes back down, she studied

The languorous gestures of the dying deposed
Dictator in his American hospital bed,
Smiling at the camera the way that Mordred smiled

Impaled on his father Arthur's spear, the Knights
All fallen, all ruin. And Mordred lifting his sword
Ran the spear's length that pierced him, and dying gave Arthur

The Dolorous Wound. The four Queens on the barge,
Argine and Palas, Morgana and Raquel,
Took Arthur aboard and away in the windy dusk.

The Queens were afraid his wound had grown too cold.
Then robbers and pillers came into the field
To take the rings and brooches and lady's favors

From off the bodies of the noble knights.
"And who were not dead all out, there they slew
To get their harness and their riches." She got

The words by heart, the noble story daring
To pillage its corpses from outside itself:
Because it could, because the loss was richer

If the world could go on ending endlessly—
Who are these pillagers, neither knight nor squire,
Like readers who enter the story at the end

Only to be read in turn, as dynasties fall
With new inheritors to loot the shell
Of each catastrophe?—the heavy balloon

Of passion escaping from the earth, but thudding
Back to transform it, like the philosopher
Who said that he could move the world itself

If he had somewhere he could stand outside it.
World without end: fifty-two weeks or cards,
But always waiting outside the deck or the year

Pillagers and witnesses, a perpetual fall:
The black captain strangles his wife, and we
In the pack applaud and applaud, the sound of our hands

In a fluttering mass around that heavy act
As in Isaiah, when after the promised End
The blessed go forth to look upon the corpses

Of the transgressors, and "their worm shall not die
Nor their fire be quenched, they shall be an abhorring
Unto flesh forever." She made it a work

Of metal nets and pouches, a spider presence.
But in her heart she felt the foretold end
Might come more lightly, even through some absurd

Miscalculation: the feeding of penicillin
Too much to pigs, so inside those heavy bodies
Unheard-of microbes would breed and multiply

To engulf the world in plague—some giddy fate
Unlikely as a perfect hand: some trick
Of Arniboule the King of Spades, the mighty

Maker and Breaker with his crown of glass
In spikes like icicles, his violent paws
Of metal, his many arms, his orbs and swords

Doubled like his reflection in the moat
Around the palace of the Moon—where now
The pair have landed with their little dog.

The back, the yoke, the yardage. Lapped seams,
The nearly invisible stitches along the collar
Turned in a sweatshop by Koreans or Malaysians

Gossiping over tea and noodles on their break
Or talking money or politics while one fitted
This armpiece with its overseam to the band

Of cuff I button at my wrist. The presser, the cutter,
The wringer, the mangle. The needle, the union,
The treadle, the bobbin. The code. The infamous blaze

At the Triangle Factory in nineteen-eleven.
One hundred and forty-six died in the flames
On the ninth floor, no hydrants, no fire escapes—

The witness in a building across the street
Who watched how a young man helped a girl to step
Up to the windowsill, then held her out

Away from the masonry wall and let her drop.
And then another. As if he were helping them up
To enter a streetcar, and not eternity.

A third before he dropped her put her arms
Around his neck and kissed him. Then he held
Her into space, and dropped her. Almost at once

He stepped to the sill himself, his jacket flared
And fluttered up from his shirt as he came down,
Air filling up the legs of his gray trousers—

Like Hart Crane's Bedlamite, "shrill shirt ballooning."
Wonderful how the pattern matches perfectly
Across the placket and over the twin bar-tacked

Corners of both pockets, like a strict rhyme
Or a major chord. Prints, plaids, checks,
Houndstooth, Tattersall, Madras. The clan tartans

Invented by mill-owners inspired by the hoax of Ossian,
To control their savage Scottish workers, tamed
By a fabricated heraldry: MacGregor,

Bailey, MacMartin. The kilt, devised for workers
To wear among the dusty clattering looms.
Weavers, carders, spinners. The loader,

The docker, the navvy. The planter, the picker, the sorter
Sweating at her machine in a litter of cotton
As slaves in calico headrags sweated in fields:

George Herbert, your descendant is a Black
Lady in South Carolina, her name is Irma
And she inspected my shirt. Its color and fit

And feel and its clean smell have satisfied
Both her and me. We have culled its cost and quality
Down to the buttons of simulated bone,

The buttonholes, the sizing, the facing, the characters
Printed in black on neckband and tail. The shape,
The label, the labor, the color, the shade. The shirt.

Some of us believe
We would have conceived romantic
Love out of our own passions
With no precedents,
Without songs and poetry—
Or have invented poetry and music
As a comb of cells for the honey.

Shaped by ignorance,
A succession of new worlds,
Congruities improvised by
Immigrants or children.

I once thought most people were Italian,
Jewish or Colored.
To be white and called
Something like *Ed Ford*
Seemed aristocratic,
A rare distinction.

Possibly I believed only gentiles
And blonds could be left-handed.

Already famous
After one year in the majors,
Whitey Ford was drafted by the Army
To play ball in the flannels
Of the Signal Corps, stationed
In Long Branch, New Jersey.

A night game, the silver potion
Of the lights, his pink skin
Shining like a burn.

Never a player
I liked or hated: a Yankee,
A mere success.

But white the chalked-off lines
In the grass, white and green
The immaculate uniform,
And white the unpigmented
Halo of his hair
When he shifted his cap:

So ordinary and distinct,
So close up, that I felt
As if I could have made him up,
Imagined him as I imagined

The ball, a scintilla
High in the black backdrop
Of the sky. Tight red stitches.
Rawlings. The bleached

Horsehide white: the color
Of nothing. Color of the past
And of the future, of the movie screen
At rest and of blank paper.

"I could have." The mind. The black
Backdrop, the white
Fly picked out by the towering
Lights. A few years later

On a blanket in the grass
By the same river
A girl and I came into
Being together
To the faint muttering
Of unthinkable
Troubadours and radios.

The emerald
Theater, the night.
Another time,
I devised a left-hander
Even more gifted
Than Whitey Ford: a Dodger.
People were amazed by him.
Once, when he was young,
He refused to pitch on Yom Kippur.

Afternoon sun on her back,
calm irregular slap
of water against a dock.

Thin pines clamber
over the hill's top—
nothing to remember,

only the same lake
that keeps making the same
sounds under her cheek

and flashing the same color.
No one to say her name,
no need, no one to praise her,

only the lake's voice—over
and over, to keep it before her.

While I lay sleeping my heart awoke.
I heard and saw but I couldn't stir.
He walked out like a man and spoke.
Though it was late
A crowd of people were awake
Strolling and talking in the street.
They greeted him and called him Coeur.
Then he was driving in a car.

He started down familiar roads.
I know the city, he was there,
But Coeur found hidden neighborhoods.
At an iron gate
That led to steps between façades
I watched him park and climb on foot
The passage to an open square
With shuttered houses and a bar,

A bright cafe where I could see
Coeur chatting with the local crowd—
Voluble heart, attentive, free,
At home, at night.
Once I think he looked back at me
And for a moment saw me wait
(I saw his face, he looked afraid)
Dreaming him from the dark outside.

"*. . . our language, forged in the dark by centuries of violent pressure, underground, out of the stuff of dead life.*"

Thirsty and languorous after their long black sleep
The old gods crooned and shuffled and shook their heads.
Dry, dry. By railroad they set out
Across the desert of stars to drink the world
Our mouths had soaked
In the strange sentences we made
While they were asleep: a pollen-tinted
Slurry of passion and lapsed
Intention, whose imagined
Taste made the savage deities hiss and snort.

In the lightless carriages, a smell of snake
And coarse fur, glands of lymphless breath
And ichor, the avid stenches of
Immortal bodies.

Their long train clicked and sighed
Through the gulfs of night between the planets
And came down through the evening fog
Of redwood canyons. From the train
At sunset, fiery warehouse windows
Along a wharf. Then dusk, a gash of neon:
Bar. Black pinewoods, a junction crossing, glimpses
Of sluggish surf among the rocks, a moan
Of dreamy forgotten divinity calling and fading
Against the windows of a town. Inside
The train, a flash
Of dragonfly wings, an antlered brow.

Black night again, and then
After the bridge, a palace on the water:

The great Refinery—impossible city of lights,
A million bulbs tracing its turreted
Boulevards and mazes. The castle of a person
Pronounced alive, the Corporation: a fictional
Lord real in law.

Barbicans and torches
Along the siding where the engine slows
At the central tanks, a ward
Of steel palisades, valved and chandeliered.

The muttering gods
Greedily penetrate those bright pavilions—
Libation of Benzene, Naphthalene, Asphalt,
Gasoline, Tar: syllables
Fractioned and cracked from unarticulated

Crude, the smeared keep of life that fed
On itself in pitchy darkness when the gods
Were new—inedible, volatile
And sublimated afresh to sting
Our tongues who use it, refined from oil of stone.

The gods batten on the vats, and drink up
Lovecries and memorized Chaucer, lines from movies
And songs hoarded in mortmain: exiles' charms,
The basal or desperate distillates of breath
Steeped, brewed and spent—
As though we were their aphids, or their bees,
That monstered up sweetness for them while they dozed.

Nothing only
what it was—

Slates, burls, rims:

Their names like the circus
Lettering on a van: *Bros.* and *Movers*,
Symmetrical buds of
Meaning in the spurs and serifs
Of scarlet with gold outlines.

Transport and Salvage,
Moving and Storage.

The house by the truck yard:
Flag walk. Shake siding. The frontyard spruce
A hilt of shadows.

And out back in the wooded lot,
The hut of scrapwood and bedframes
Lashed with housewire by children,
Hitchknots of the plainsman
Or the plasterer shoring a ladder.

Cache of cigarettes, tongue
And groove, magazines,
Chocolate, books: *Moaning she guided*

His throbbing manhood and *Southwark Bridge*
Which is of iron
And London Bridge which is of stone.

Hobo cookery in tin cans.
Muffled coherence like dreams.

Printslugs,
Glass insulators, "Enemy Zeros."
Maimed mouth-harp and sashweight.
Trojans and Sheiks,

Esquire,
Beaverboard, Romex.
Each thing or name a river
With a silty bottom.
The source hidden, the mouth
Emptying in the ocean.

Hut as of driftwood,
Scavengers and Haulers,
Household and Commercial Removals.
Westphal's Auxiliator, *quim, poorhouse,*
Homasote,

The mighty forest of significance—
Possibly dreamed
By a man in Headlight overalls,
Even by the one we found
Sleeping there once
With his empty of Seven
Crown, not necessarily
By a god or goddess—
The embroidered letters
HEAD tapering each smaller and LIGHT

Each larger, like beams thrown
From the center—that snoring,
Historical heart.

Foundry of the dead, the dead invisible hammer
Forgotten that dropped to forge
The ring behind the doorknob: brass roses
The trade tongue calls them, and forges the words—
Tongue, strike-plate, shaft, escutcheon, exhaling tarnish
Onto your hand that reaches unknowing toward them
Over and over in doorways and all but touches.

Shaft and claw, clangor and fission:
The brazen tongue of Babylon.

The faint implacable hammer behind the hammer
Homing the die and bevel and framing the house.

Hammerdust air, a contagious powder of blows.

Mattock that breaks the earth.
Sacrifice, felling the housel.

At the window
Where children are walking home from school it showers
Around their heads: the burst of particles that spray
Up from the anvil unnoticed over the children
And onto the window—sash, lights, mullion and sill,
Molecules that gild the panes and film the moist
Pupil of the eye with ashy silver.

Airhammer in the street
Tireless and violent in a fissure
Of pavement. Warhammer of Tristram or Shiva.

Old hammer of mortal perfection, idolatrous hammer
Of golden calves and birds, the shingle maker
Wielding his maul and froe, dead jeweler's hammer
Forcing a braid of silver into the vessels
Of living bodies, heartworm
Tendrils and cilia. Shapes taken out of nature
In wires of laurel or olive. Roses.

Pounding: the bell-shaped strokes.

Oh heavy swollen pump, the urgent pressure
Lifted in desire.

Hammer of love hammered by the hammer of words.

Futile the prophet Ezekiel's curse on the sledge
Hefted by the weary idol-smith who works
Hypnotized faint with hunger beyond his supper
By lamplight, thirsty, and beyond his death
Lifting the ponderous shaper.

In his anger
Ezekiel said to smear the bread in the ovens
With Babylonian shit, as a mouth penance
For graving images, but the very baker
Pounded and pounded the dough and twisted the
Ropes of the bread of affliction
Into crown-shaped loaves.

Braids, images.

Blind tool of perfection, bludgeon
Handed from the dead who drive you
Hand on the doorknob between Sheol and Creation,
Stalled on the threshold, unable to cross.

Pounding of the heart,
Inherited drum of the doorway.

Mattock of want, sickle of Kali, bare hand
Of hunger—you too have lifted it and let it fall,
You have committed images, the tool
Is warm from your hand.

In the willows along the river at Pleasure Bay
A catbird singing, never the same phrase twice.
Here under the pines a little off the road
In 1927 the Chief of Police
And Mrs. W. killed themselves together,
Sitting in a roadster. Ancient unshaken pilings
And underwater chunks of still-mortared brick
In shapes like bits of puzzle strew the bottom
Where the landing was for Price's Hotel and Theater.
And here's where boats blew two blasts for the keeper
To shunt the iron swing-bridge. He leaned on the gears
Like a skipper in the hut that housed the works
And the bridge moaned and turned on its middle pier
To let them through. In the middle of the summer
Two or three cars might wait for the iron trusswork
Winching aside, with maybe a child to notice
A name on the stern in black-and-gold on white,
Sandpiper, Patsy Ann, Do Not Disturb,
The Idler. If a boat was running whiskey,
The bridge clanged shut behind it as it passed
And opened up again for the Coast Guard cutter
Slowly as a sundial, and always jammed halfway.
The roadbed whole, but opened like a switch,
The river pulling and coursing between the piers.
Never the same phrase twice, the catbird filling
The humid August evening near the inlet
With borrowed music that he melds and changes.
Dragonflies and sandflies, frogs in the rushes, two bodies

Not moving in the open car among the pines,
A sliver of story. The tenor at Price's Hotel,
In clown costume, unfurls the sorrow gathered
In ruffles at his throat and cuffs, high quavers
That hold like splashes of light on the dark water,
The aria's closing phrases, changed and fading.
And after a gap of quiet, cheers and applause
Audible in the houses across the river,
Some in the audience weeping as if they had melted
Inside the music. Never the same. In Berlin
The daughter of an English lord, in love
With Adolf Hitler, whom she has met. She is taking
Possession of the apartment of a couple,
Elderly well-off Jews. They survive the war
To settle here in the Bay, the old lady
Teaches piano, but the whole world swivels
And gapes at their feet as the girl and a high-up Nazi
Examine the furniture, the glass, the pictures,
The elegant story that was theirs and now
Is a part of hers. A few months later the English
Enter the war and she shoots herself in a park,
An addled, upper-class girl, her life that passes
Into the lives of others or into a place.
The taking of lives—the Chief and Mrs. W.
Took theirs to stay together, as local ghosts.
Last flurries of kisses, the revolver's barrel,
Shivers of a story that a child might hear
And half remember, voices in the rushes,
A singing in the willows. From across the river,
Faint quavers of music, the same phrase twice and again,
Ranging and building. Over the high new bridge
The flashing of traffic homeward from the racetrack,
With one boat chugging under the arches, outward
Unnoticed through Pleasure Bay to the open sea.
Here's where the people stood to watch the theater
Burn on the water. All that night the fireboats

Kept playing their spouts of water into the blaze.
In the morning, smoking pilasters and beams.
Black smell of char for weeks, the ruin already
Soaking back into the river. After you die
You hover near the ceiling above your body
And watch the mourners awhile. A few days more
You float above the heads of the ones you knew
And watch them through a twilight. As it grows darker
You wander off and find your way to the river
And wade across. On the other side, night air,
Willows, the smell of the river, and a mass
Of sleeping bodies all along the bank,
A kind of singing from among the rushes
Calling you further forward in the dark.
You lie down and embrace one body, the limbs
Heavy with sleep reach eagerly up around you
And you make love until your soul brims up
And burns free out of you and shifts and spills
Down over into that other body, and you
Forget the life you had and begin again
On the same crossing—maybe as a child who passes
Through the same place. But never the same way twice.
Here in the daylight, the catbird in the willows,
The new cafe, with a terrace and a landing,
Frogs in the cattails where the swing-bridge was—
Here's where you might have slipped across the water
When you were only a presence, at Pleasure Bay.